Cooking with Dad

Judy Bastyra

Drawings by Paul Daviz

BLOOMSBURY

To Colonel Jam Jar with love from Olive.

First published in Great Britain in 1996
by Bloomsbury Children's Books,
2 Soho Square, London W1V 6HB

Copyright © 1996 Judy Bastyra
Illustrations © 1996 Paul Daviz
Designer: Lisa Coombes

A CIP catalogue record for this book is
available from the British Library.

ISBN 0-7475-2523-4

10 9 8 7 6 5 4 3 2 1
Printed and bound in Great Britain by
Butler & Tanner Ltd, Frome and London

Contents

INTRODUCTION 4

TOOLS, TERMS & MEASURES 5

DAD CAN'T EVEN BOIL AN EGG 6

HE AIN'T HEAVY, HE'S MY DAD! 10

SPAGHETTI WITH ATTITUDE 14

MACHINE MAGIC 19

GRAZING AND GAZING 24

GAMES TO PLAY AND EAT 30

MY DAD'S A CARNIVORE! 35

THE GREAT OUTDOORS 40

COOKING FOR MUM 46

TASTE BUDDIES OF THE ORIENT 51

WASHING UP IS A DRAG 56

TAKING DAD SHOPPING 59

WHY CAN'T WE EAT AFTERS BEFORE? 61

INDEX 64

Introduction

When I was a little girl my dad worked during the week. The only opportunity he had to spend time in the kitchen was at the weekends and that is when I learned about *Cooking with Dad*. He could only cook two dishes – scrambled eggs and grilled chops. I helped him by cooking toast for the eggs and slicing tomatoes to eat with the chops. Sometimes they worked out, but often they didn't and I always wished he knew how to cook some other dishes. Even so, what we cooked tasted good because we had cooked it together and it was my special time with my dad.

Now, of course, he's rather bored with scrambled eggs and chops and wishes he had learned to cook other things. So, I decided to write a book for all the dads and kids who want to learn how to cook lots of different and delicious dishes while spending time together, having fun in the kitchen.

As you become more practised as a cook, you will soon be able to work out how to adjust the quantities and ingredients given in recipes to suit your family. And I hope you'll soon be inventing recipes of your own.

Cooking can be Dangerous

This symbol in a recipe is to remind you to be especially careful. But you *always* need to take care when handling hot dishes, sharp knives, electrical equipment, and around the barbecue or Hungi fire. Dad or another adult should be present whenever you are cooking.

Always wear oven gloves when handling hot dishes. Oven gloves are not what ovens wear in the winter, they're padded gloves to protect your hands.

Sharp knives are particularly dangerous, so be extra careful when cutting and chopping because bits of finger don't taste very nice in the chilli!

Keep a separate chopping board for meat and poultry. Wear rubber gloves and scrub the board well with very hot water after you use it. This is called *germ warfare*!

Always wash fruit and vegetables well before you eat or cook them.

Don't forget to clear up after you cook, otherwise Mum may be dangerous!

Before you Begin

Wash your hands.
Put on an apron.
Clean the work surface (especially if it's where your pets like to take a stroll or you've just fixed your bike on it!).

Tools, Terms and Measures

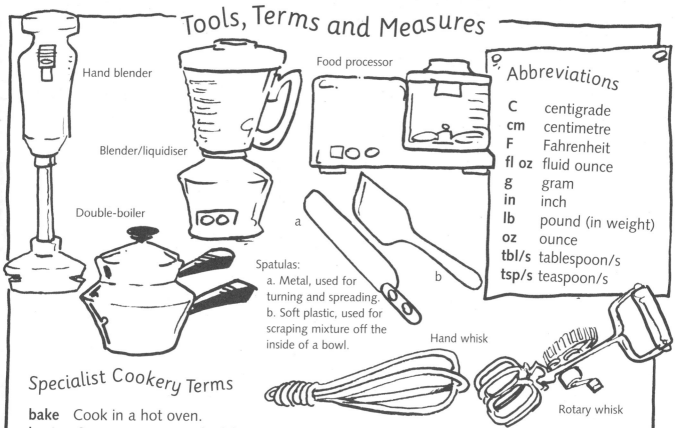

Hand blender

Blender/liquidiser

Double-boiler

Food processor

Spatulas:
a. Metal, used for turning and spreading.
b. Soft plastic, used for scraping mixture off the inside of a bowl.

Hand whisk

Rotary whisk

Abbreviations

C	centigrade
cm	centimetre
F	Fahrenheit
fl oz	fluid ounce
g	gram
in	inch
lb	pound (in weight)
oz	ounce
tbl/s	tablespoon/s
tsp/s	teaspoon/s

Specialist Cookery Terms

bake   Cook in a hot oven.

baste   Spoon sauce or melted fat over food to prevent it drying out during cooking.

batter   Runny mixture made by beating together flour, egg, and milk or water.

cream   Mix butter and sugar to a creamy consistency.

fold   Gently add an ingredient so as to mix it in without stirring or beating.

knead   Work dough by stretching and folding it until it is smooth and shiny.

marinate   Soak food in a spicy sauce to absorb extra flavour.

preheat oven   Allow 30 minutes to heat up to required temperature.

purée   Cooked fruit or vegetables blended or sieved to a fine pulp.

season   Add salt, pepper, herbs and spices.

score   Cut or scratch surface without cutting right through it.

simmer   Cook liquid without allowing it to boil.

stir-fry   Fry food (usually in a wok) while stirring constantly.

DAD CAN'T EVEN BOIL AN EGG

Most men nowadays can cook but if your dad can't, it's time he learnt. He'll enjoy cooking, as well as eating, if you show him how much fun you can have cooking together. The easiest way to start is with an egg.

How to boil an egg

You can boil an egg in two ways. **1**. If it has come straight out of the fridge, put it into into a saucepan of cold water and bring to the boil. **2**. If the egg has been kept at room temperature, gently lower it into boiling water with a long-handled spoon. And to cook your egg just the way you like it, start timing it once the water comes to the boil.

Medium-boiled (firm white, slightly set yolk)
Sizes 1–3: 5 minutes.   Sizes 4–7: 4 minutes
Hard-boiled (firm white, just-set slightly floury yolk)
Sizes 1–3: 10 minutes.   Sizes 4–7: 8–9 minutes.

How to crack a hard-boiled egg
Play catch with it!

COOK'S TIP
For hard-boiled eggs with no black ring around the yolk, rinse them under cold water until they are cool enough to handle.

6

Funny Fried Eggs

Eggs can be fried in different sorts of fat. Use a good quality vegetable oil (soya sunflower, or olive), or butter, ghee, margarine, dripping or bacon fat. Butter is delicious but oil is healthier.

If you want your egg to have a funny shape, fry it inside a metal biscuit cutter. Place the cutter in the frying pan. Add and heat the oil, then crack an egg into it.

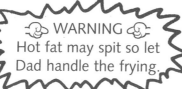

WARNING
Hot fat may spit so let Dad handle the frying.

For a regular fried egg, gently heat a small amount of oil in a frying pan. Crack egg into the hot oil and baste (spoon hot fat over it). Cook until the underneath is firm (2–3 minutes). To cook the yolk through but keep it runny, cover the pan with a lid for a few minutes.

Daddy's Fried Eggs

If you don't have a metal biscuit cutter, fold a slice of bread in half and take a bite out of the centre. Heat a dab of butter and a tablespoon of oil in the pan. Carefully put the bread in the hot fat and fry on one side until crispy brown. Turn it over with an egg slice, then crack an egg into the centre of the bread. Fry for 2–3 minutes.

Meringues (pronounced mer-angs)

Everyone thinks making meringues must be difficult but it is really easy if you use clean, dry beaters and bowl, and beat the egg white a lot. They don't work if they haven't been beaten enough, or if the mixture contains even the smallest amount of fat or egg yolk. The hardest thing about making meringues is separating the egg from the white.

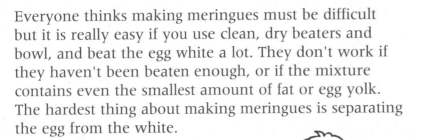

INGREDIENTS

Makes about 24
6 egg whites
Pinch of salt
350 g (12 oz)
caster sugar

Have two clean dry mixing bowls ready.

1. Tap the egg sharply on the edge of a bowl. This may need practice!

2. Hold the cracked egg over a mixing bowl and gently ease the shell apart.

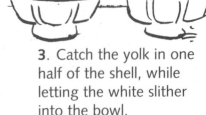

3. Catch the yolk in one half of the shell, while letting the white slither into the bowl.

4. Transfer the yolk from one half of the shell to the other, until all the white is in the bowl.

5. Drop the yolk into the other bowl.

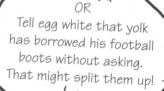

OR
Tell egg white that yolk has borrowed his football boots without asking. That might split them up!

1. Set the oven to 110°C (225°F) or gas mark ¼. Line a baking tray with baking parchment.

2. Add salt to the egg whites and whisk until they become stiff. An electric whisk makes this job easy. You can use a hand whisk but it takes longer. The mixture is ready if it stands up in a peak when you lift the whisk out of the bowl.

3. Whisk about half the sugar into the egg whites. Use a metal spoon or a flat-bladed knife to fold the rest of the sugar into the mixture. You might think it's pretty silly trying to *fold* sugar. What it really means is to *gently mix in*.

4. Drop tablespoonfuls of the mixture on to the lined baking tray, so they are not touching. Try to turn the spoon each time so that the meringue twirls up into a peak.

5. Place the tray in the warm oven for about 3 hours. Set oven timer, an alarm clock or watch. Meringues need to cook slowly, or they become all soggy inside. If you try to hurry them by increasing the heat, they quickly burn and become sticky. When cooked, they should feel firm and lift away easily from the baking parchment. Leave them to cool on a wire rack. Any you don't eat, store in an airtight container.

For a special treat, sandwich two together with whipped cream.

What to do with six egg yolks

You'll have plenty of time to wash up while the meringues are cooking, and to whip up something delicious with the left-over yolks. There isn't space here for more recipes, so look up *Crème Anglais*, *Crème Brûlèe* and *Egg Custard* in other books.

HE AIN'T HEAVY, HE'S MY DAD!

I love food like chips and sweets but aren't they bad for me?

A little bit of what you fancy does you good.

Most of us love fried foods, puddings and sweets. They're only fattening and bad for us if we eat too much of them every day.

Dads usually have more time to cook at weekends. If yours gets up late, he could combine breakfast and lunch and make pancakes for brunch. American pancakes are small, round and fluffy and served in stacks. English ones are large, floppy, and served one at a time.

HEALTH HINT
After a big meal, go to the park together. You'll need the exercise to work up an appetite for the next one!

The Great Brunch Munch

Try *Pigs in a Blanket.* (See page 13.)

OINK!

Or even a huge steak for breakfast?

Or crispy sweet-cured bacon with melon.

American Pancakes

1. Heat oven to 110°C (225°F) or gas mark ¼, to keep pancakes hot.

2. Sift into a bowl, the flour, salt, sugar and baking powder. Make a well in the centre.

3. Mix eggs and 240 ml (8 fl oz) of the milk. Pour it into the dry ingredients. Mix quickly together and add melted butter. If batter is too thick, add the extra milk. Cover and set aside for at least 1 hour.

4. Lightly grease frying pan with some oil or butter, and heat. Dad can sprinkle a few drops of water into pan. If they bounce, it is hot enough.

5. Pour 2 tablespoons of batter into the pan and cook 1-2 minutes, until surface bubbles begin to break. Turn over with a spatula. Cook a minute until underside is golden brown. Serve at once or keep warm on a baking tray in oven until you've made enough for everyone. Don't stack them, they'll go flabby.

Secrets of Successful Pancakes

- Add wet ingredients to the dry ones, quickly.
- Don't over-beat.
- Let mixture stand 1-3 hours before cooking.
- Only turn a pancake over once.

panic Box

The first pancake may be a disaster! Sometimes the frying pan forgets how to make them. After one, it will miraculously remember.

INGREDIENTS

Makes 12-14 pancakes
350 g (12 oz) plain flour
1 tsp salt
2 tbls sugar
2 tsps baking powder
2 eggs, beaten
300-360 ml (10-12 fl oz) milk
3 tbls melted butter or oil, plus some for cooking

English Pancakes

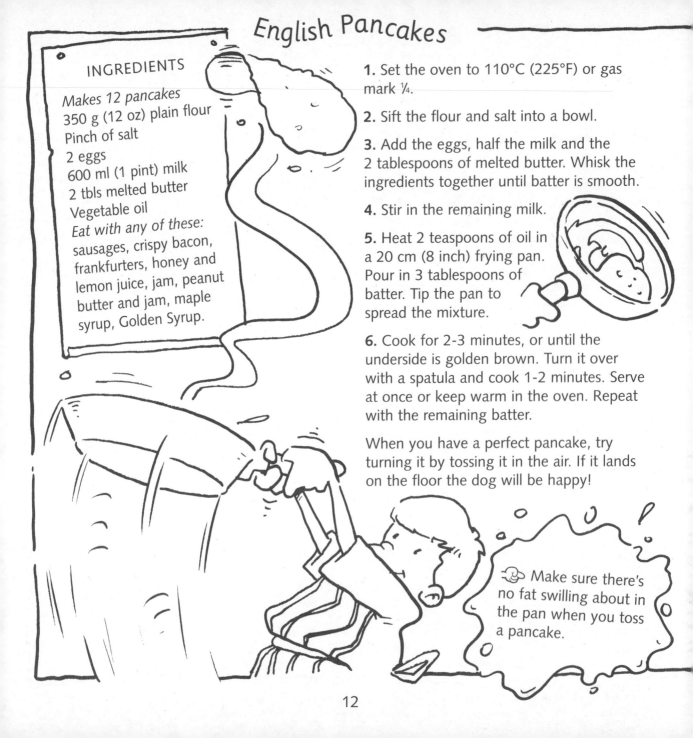

INGREDIENTS

Makes 12 pancakes
350 g (12 oz) plain flour
Pinch of salt
2 eggs
600 ml (1 pint) milk
2 tbls melted butter
Vegetable oil
Eat with any of these:
sausages, crispy bacon, frankfurters, honey and lemon juice, jam, peanut butter and jam, maple syrup, Golden Syrup.

1. Set the oven to 110°C (225°F) or gas mark ¼.

2. Sift the flour and salt into a bowl.

3. Add the eggs, half the milk and the 2 tablespoons of melted butter. Whisk the ingredients together until batter is smooth.

4. Stir in the remaining milk.

5. Heat 2 teaspoons of oil in a 20 cm (8 inch) frying pan. Pour in 3 tablespoons of batter. Tip the pan to spread the mixture.

6. Cook for 2-3 minutes, or until the underside is golden brown. Turn it over with a spatula and cook 1-2 minutes. Serve at once or keep warm in the oven. Repeat with the remaining batter.

When you have a perfect pancake, try turning it by tossing it in the air. If it lands on the floor the dog will be happy!

Make sure there's no fat swilling about in the pan when you toss a pancake.

Pigs in the Blanket

Grill some sausages then wrap each one in a pancake and serve with maple or Golden syrup. English pancakes are best for *Pigs in a Blanket*.

Dad's Special Tip(ple)

Substitute beer for half the milk in the pancake mixture. Dads can drink the left-over beer while they're cooking.

French Toast For Four

1. Set the oven to 110°C (225°F) or gas mark ¼.

2. Beat eggs, milk, vanilla essence and sugar together in a wide bowl.

3. Dip slices of bread into the mixture. Stir to let mixture soak into surface.

4. Heat a frying pan. When it's hot add a little butter. Add soaked slices of bread, one or two at a time. Fry for 3-4 minutes until light brown. Turn with a spatula and cook 2-3 minutes. Remove from pan and keep warm in the oven until ready to serve. Don't stack them.

Dad's Bistro
INGREDIENTS

6 eggs
2 tbls milk
¼ tsp vanilla essence
1 tsp sugar
8 slices thickly-sliced bread, brioche loaf, or Cholla
2 tbls butter or oil

13

SPAGHETTI WITH ATTITUDE

I hate eating with the baby, he makes such a mess.

Most grown-ups (and older brothers and sisters!) don't want children to make a mess at the table, even though they might quite like to themselves. You need to know how to eat politely if you go to a friend's house and, one day, you may even be invited to a banquet at the palace! Here's your chance to make a mess without anyone fussing about manners.

I know. But he does enjoy himself. Why don't we all make a mess together. Let's cook **Spaghetti With Attitude!**

Ways to eat spaghetti

- With no hands.
- Suck in strand by strand.

- On toast.
- Twirled around a fork. Practise this, in case you have to eat in public.

Here's how . . .

1. Plunge a fork into the spaghetti and twirl it to secure a few strands.

3. When spaghetti is wound into a bite-size ball, fork it into your mouth.

2. Put the fork in the centre of a spoon and continue twirling.

Cooking Spaghetti

Spaghetti is long pasta. Always choose the longest for maximum mess. Never cut up your spaghetti – either twirl it, or suck it up a strand at a time, making disgusting slurping noises.

1. Bring a large pan of lightly salted water to a rolling boil. Add a few drops of oil to prevent the pasta sticking to itself. 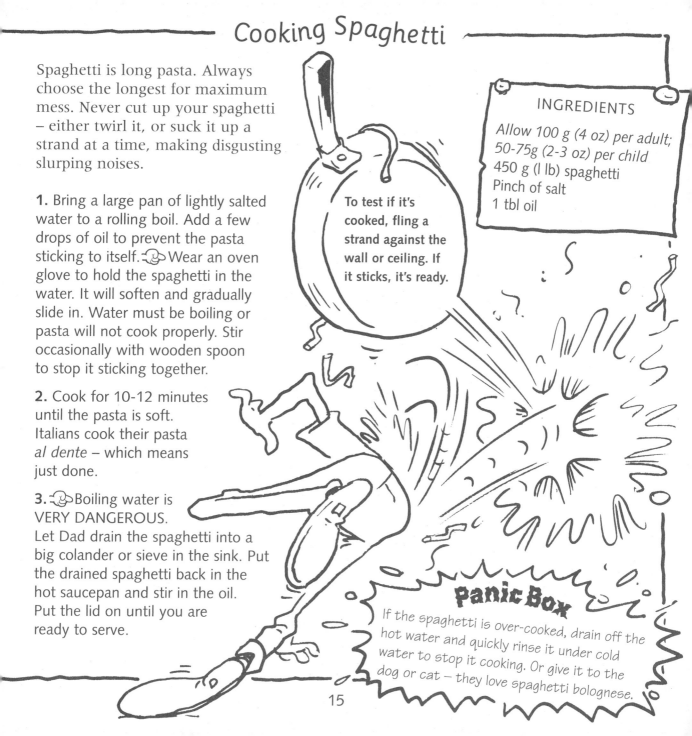 Wear an oven glove to hold the spaghetti in the water. It will soften and gradually slide in. Water must be boiling or pasta will not cook properly. Stir occasionally with wooden spoon to stop it sticking together.

2. Cook for 10-12 minutes until the pasta is soft. Italians cook their pasta *al dente* – which means just done.

3. Boiling water is VERY DANGEROUS. Let Dad drain the spaghetti into a big colander or sieve in the sink. Put the drained spaghetti back in the hot saucepan and stir in the oil. Put the lid on until you are ready to serve.

To test if it's cooked, fling a strand against the wall or ceiling. If it sticks, it's ready.

INGREDIENTS

Allow 100 g (4 oz) per adult;
50-75g (2-3 oz) per child
450 g (l lb) spaghetti
Pinch of salt
1 tbl oil

panic Box

If the spaghetti is over-cooked, drain off the hot water and quickly rinse it under cold water to stop it cooking. Or give it to the dog or cat – they love spaghetti bolognese.

Tomato Sauce

Everyone should know how to cook this. If you can cook a good tomato sauce you will never be bored with food because you can make all sorts of other dishes by adding some extra ingredients.

1. Heat the oil in a saucepan. Add the onion and fry over moderate heat for 5-7 minutes until the onion is soft and translucent but not brown. Add the garlic and cook for a further 2 minutes.

2. Stir in chopped tomatoes, tomato purée, oregano, sugar, salt and black pepper. Bring to the boil. Lower the heat and simmer (mixture moves but doesn't boil) over low heat for about 15 minutes. Stir from time to time.

3. Serve on top of spaghetti. It tastes excellent with a sprinkling of Parmesan or Cheddar cheese.

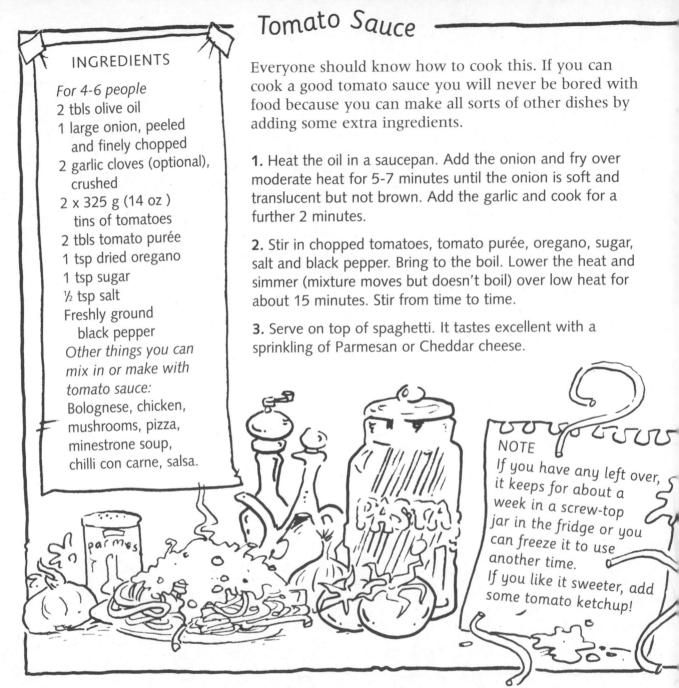

NOTE
If you have any left over, it keeps for about a week in a screw-top jar in the fridge or you can freeze it to use another time.
If you like it sweeter, add some tomato ketchup!

Spaghetti Bolognese for Four

One of the best meals in the world is Spaghetti Bolognese. It's a great favourite for all the family and is guaranteed to make a big mess in the slurping race.

1. Heat the oil in a saucepan, add the onion and garlic and fry over moderate heat for 5 minutes. Add the meat and stir until the meat has browned.

2. Stir in the chopped tomatoes. Sprinkle in the stock cube and add the Worcestershire sauce, basil, bay leaf, salt, pepper and water.

3. Bring to the boil. Reduce the heat, cover the pan and simmer gently for 20 minutes, stirring from time to time.

4. Remove the bay leaf before you serve with spaghetti.

INGREDIENTS

2 tbls oil
1 onion, finely chopped
1 garlic clove
450 g (1 lb) lean
   minced beef
325 g (14 oz) fresh or
   tinned tomatoes
Beef stock cube
1 tbls Worcestershire
   sauce
1 tsp dried basil
1 bay leaf
½ tsp salt
Freshly ground black
   pepper
300 ml (½ pint) water

Rules for Spaghetti slurping race

You have 5 minutes to make as much mess as you can. The person who gets the messiest is the winner.

1. You are allowed one spear at the spaghetti each go.

2. Each player has 20 goes.

3. If you bite the spaghetti you are disqualified.

Coloured Worms with Jam

The best pasta to use for this dish is vermicelli (which in Italian means little worms!).

1. Cook the vermicelli in lots of boiling water for 7-8 minutes. After Dad drains it, he should divide it into three separate bowls.

2. While vermicelli is still hot, add blue food colouring to one bowl, red to another, and leave the third its natural colour.

3. Gently stir the Vermicelli in the first two bowls until it is well coloured.

4. Spoon some of each of the worms on to plates and serve with your favourite jam.

INGREDIENTS

For 4 people
225 g (8 oz) dried vermicelli
1 tsp blue food colouring
1 tsp red food colouring
4 tbls jam

Strawberry

MACHINE MAGIC

Power tools and electronic kitchen gadgetry can be very dangerous but they make great noises and do speed things up, especially when you're cooking. It's easy to whip up salsa in a blender, make a 5-minute dessert in a microwave, or even whiz up a creamy soup without even taking it out of its saucepan.

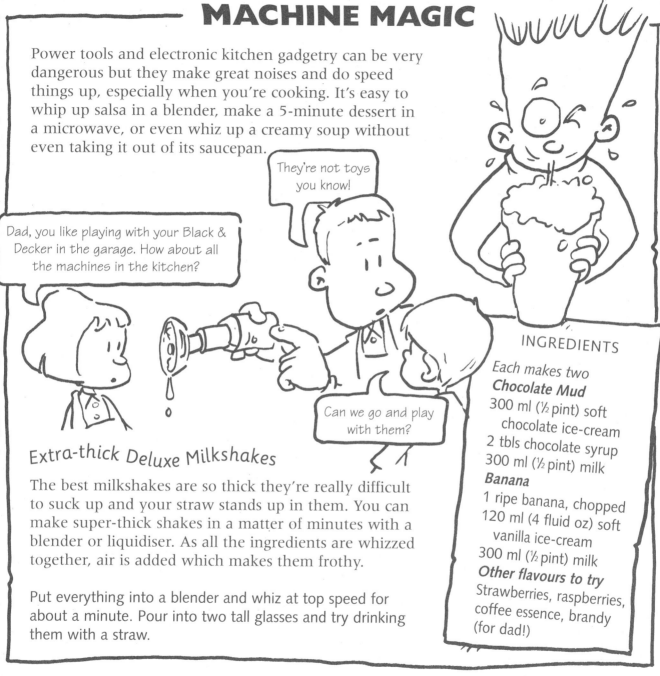

They're not toys you know!

Dad, you like playing with your Black & Decker in the garage. How about all the machines in the kitchen?

Can we go and play with them?

Extra-thick Deluxe Milkshakes

The best milkshakes are so thick they're really difficult to suck up and your straw stands up in them. You can make super-thick shakes in a matter of minutes with a blender or liquidiser. As all the ingredients are whizzed together, air is added which makes them frothy.

Put everything into a blender and whiz at top speed for about a minute. Pour into two tall glasses and try drinking them with a straw.

INGREDIENTS

Each makes two
Chocolate Mud
300 ml (½ pint) soft chocolate ice-cream
2 tbls chocolate syrup
300 ml (½ pint) milk
Banana
1 ripe banana, chopped
120 ml (4 fluid oz) soft vanilla ice-cream
300 ml (½ pint) milk
Other flavours to try
Strawberries, raspberries, coffee essence, brandy (for dad!)

Food Processors

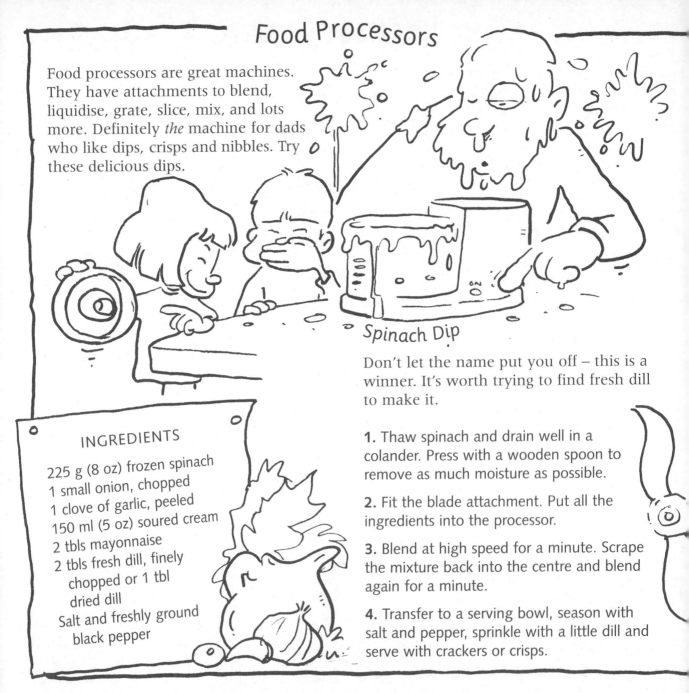

Food processors are great machines. They have attachments to blend, liquidise, grate, slice, mix, and lots more. Definitely *the* machine for dads who like dips, crisps and nibbles. Try these delicious dips.

Spinach Dip

Don't let the name put you off – this is a winner. It's worth trying to find fresh dill to make it.

1. Thaw spinach and drain well in a colander. Press with a wooden spoon to remove as much moisture as possible.

2. Fit the blade attachment. Put all the ingredients into the processor.

3. Blend at high speed for a minute. Scrape the mixture back into the centre and blend again for a minute.

4. Transfer to a serving bowl, season with salt and pepper, sprinkle with a little dill and serve with crackers or crisps.

INGREDIENTS

225 g (8 oz) frozen spinach
1 small onion, chopped
1 clove of garlic, peeled
150 ml (5 oz) soured cream
2 tbls mayonnaise
2 tbls fresh dill, finely chopped or 1 tbl dried dill
Salt and freshly ground black pepper

White Bean Dip

This delicious dip can be used as a topping for baked potatoes or with salad as a filling in hot pitta bread. You can use this recipe to make other bean dips, by using black-eyed, red kidney, or butter beans.

1. Fit the blade attachment. Drain the beans and tip them into the food processor.

2. Add the onion, garlic, lemon juice, olive oil, half the parsley, and season with salt and black pepper.

3. Blend for 30 seconds, scrape the mixture down and blend for another 30 seconds.

4. Transfer to a serving bowl and sprinkle with parsley. Dip into it with crisps, slices of pitta bread or carrot sticks.

INGREDIENTS

400 g (12 oz) tinned cannellini beans
½ small onion, chopped
1 garlic clove, peeled
1 tbl fresh lemon juice
2 tbls olive oil
Salt and freshly ground black pepper
1 tbl fresh basil, finely chopped; or 1 tsp dried
1 tbl fresh parsley, finely chopped

Hand-held Blenders

An excellent time-saving machine is a hand-held blender. It can be used straight into the saucepan (less to wash up!). You can use it to make sauces and gravies, whiz up hot milky drinks, and it's brilliant for making soups.

Creamy Leek and Potato Soup

In France this is called Vichyssoise (pronounced vishy-swarze) and is often served cold, but it's good hot. You can make lots of cream soups like this, using other vegetables instead of leeks.

INGREDIENTS

450 g (1 lb) leeks
50 g (2 oz) butter
2 tbls olive or sunflower oil
2 large potatoes
½ tsp curry powder
½ tsp salt
Freshly ground black pepper
900 ml (1½ pints) chicken stock,
   or stock cube and water
300 m (½ pint) full cream milk
150 m (5 fl oz) double cream

1. Leeks are always full of grit. Cut them lengthways down one side and wash them well in cold water. Slice and leave them to drain in a colander.

2. Wash and chop the potatoes into small cubes.

3. Melt the butter and oil in a large saucepan. Add leeks and potatoes. Cook gently for 10 minutes, turning constantly with a wooden spoon.

4. Stir in curry powder, salt and pepper and add the chicken stock. Bring to the boil, reduce heat, cover the pan and cook for 20 minutes until the vegetables are soft.

5. Set aside to cool a little *before* Dad blends the vegetables and stock for about 3 minutes in the pan. When smooth and creamy, stir in the milk. Taste and add more seasoning if you wish.

6. Reheat the soup gently. Serve with a little cream swirled into each bowl.

panic Box

Switch off the machine before you lift it out of the pan, or you'll have a faceful of mashed leek and potato and glistening globules of it splattered all over the kitchen.

Microwaves

In a house where a lot of people come home hungry at different times, a microwave is very useful for hot meals within minutes. They're really good to heat food and drinks, like hot chocolate, and for ultra-fast baked potatoes and corn on the cob. They're not dangerous for kids to use – but be careful not to burn yourself when removing a hot dish.

Cooking Times

Corn on the cob: 4 minutes on high.

Baked potatoes: 8 minutes on high.

Hot chocolate: 2 minutes on high. Transfer to a cool mug before drinking it.

Microwave tips

• Microwaves can be a serious hazard to anyone with a pacemaker.

• Never use metal objects (or china with metal trims).

• Always use microwavable cling film.

• Use kitchen paper to wrap potatoes.

INGREDIENTS

225 g (8 oz) digestive biscuits

75 g (3 oz) unsalted butter

410 ml (12 fl oz) sweetened condensed milk

600 ml (1 pint) strawberry yoghurt

Fresh sliced strawberries

Super-quick Chiffon Pie

If you want a super-sweet pudding, this is for you.

1. Make the base by crumbling biscuits into a bowl. Melt and pour in the butter. Mix well. Spread it in a microwavable pie dish. Refrigerate for 10 minutes.

2. Mix the condensed milk and yoghurt together in a bowl and pour it over the biscuit base.

3. Microwave on high for 6-8 minutes.

4. Remove, allow to cool and set. Decorate with sliced strawberries.

GRAZING AND GAZING

What can we eat while we slob out in front of the telly?

Mum doesn't like us eating in there.

She's right, but it's OK as a treat if we want to watch a special programme together.

Eating in front of the television is fun when you all want to watch a favourite programme. But mealtimes are important because it's the one time each day for families to talk about what they've been doing or want to do. They're a good time to settle arguments too!

For trouble-free TV eating

- Nothing that can spill, stain or stick.
- Damp cloth nearby in case of accidents.
- Food you can eat with your fingers.
- Check the length of time your favourite TV programme takes, then plan what you're going to cook to fit in with it. You won't want to be standing over a hot oven just when a winning goal is being played.

Giant Hero Sandwich for Six

A great meal to prepare for uninterrupted TV viewing is a giant sandwich. Buy the longest, crunchiest baguette (French bread) you can find and pack it with your favourite sandwich fillings. The secret of a winning Hero is to pull out the soft doughy bread inside to make room for more filling.

INGREDIENTS

1 large French stick
Margarine or butter
3 tomatoes, sliced
Lettuce leaves, shredded
¼ cucumber, sliced
100 g (4 oz) sliced cheese
100 (4 oz) honey roast ham
100 g (4 oz) salami or mortadella
100 g (4 oz) chicken or turkey
Mayonnaise (and mustard)
Salt and pepper to taste

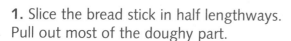

1. Slice the bread stick in half lengthways. Pull out most of the doughy part.

2. Butter the bread. Fill one half with alternate layers of salad, sliced meat and cheese. Spread mayonnaise over each layer of salad. Layers should be piled up quite high. Season with salt, pepper and mustard to taste.

3. Cover with the other half of the loaf. Wrap in cling film until you're ready to eat.

4. Serve on a large bread board so everyone can cut off as much as they want.

Nachos

Nachos are really cool. In America they are *the* Tex-Mex (Texan-Mexican) status snack. Buy a packet of tortilla chips, add lots of cheese, some pickled chilli if you like it hot, some guacamole (avocado dip) and pig out hombre! For telly watching build a giant Nacho stack to share.

INGREDIENTS

1 packet tortilla corn chips
225 g (8 oz) Cheddar cheese
Serve with
Sour cream
Guacamole (see recipe)
Tomato salsa (see page 28)

1. Preheat oven to 220°C (425°F) or gas mark 7.

2. Shake a layer of chips on to an oven-proof serving dish. Sprinkle with grated cheese. Keep adding layers of chips and cheese until they're all used up.

3. Bake in the oven for 3-5 minutes until the cheese is just melted.

4. Serve with guacamole, salsa and sour cream.

Guacamole (Avocado Dip)

It's easy to make guacamole. You can make it a few hours ahead but it tastes better if served immediately.

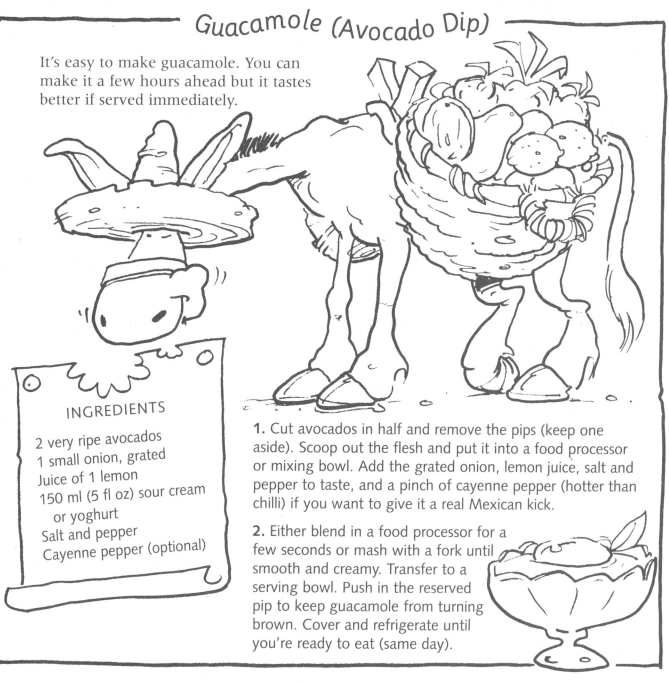

INGREDIENTS

2 very ripe avocados
1 small onion, grated
Juice of 1 lemon
150 ml (5 fl oz) sour cream
    or yoghurt
Salt and pepper
Cayenne pepper (optional)

1. Cut avocados in half and remove the pips (keep one aside). Scoop out the flesh and put it into a food processor or mixing bowl. Add the grated onion, lemon juice, salt and pepper to taste, and a pinch of cayenne pepper (hotter than chilli) if you want to give it a real Mexican kick.

2. Either blend in a food processor for a few seconds or mash with a fork until smooth and creamy. Transfer to a serving bowl. Push in the reserved pip to keep guacamole from turning brown. Cover and refrigerate until you're ready to eat (same day).

Mexican Salsa

WARNING
Wear rubber gloves when you de-seed chillies – they're not only hot to eat, they sting like mad if you get your hands near your eyes or mouth!

INGREDIENTS

2 tbls chopped onion
450 g (1 lb) tomatoes, chopped
1 green chilli (optional)
2 tbls fresh coriander leaves
1 tsp sugar
½ tsp salt
1 tbl fresh lime juice

1. Slice along one side of the chilli and scrape out the seeds. Rinse, then chop the chilli.

2. Put all the ingredients into a food processor and whiz on high for 30 seconds.

3. Transfer to a serving bowl. Cover and refrigerate for 30 minutes to let the flavours mingle.

Chilli Con Carne for Eight

Another Tex-Mex dish ideal for gazing and grazing is Chilli Con Carne. Basically it's beef and red kidney beans in a spicy tomato sauce. It doesn't have to be too spicy hot.

1. Heat the oil in a large saucepan over medium heat. Add the onion and garlic and cook for 5 minutes.

2. Add the meat and cook for 5 minutes, stirring until evenly browned.

3. Add chopped tomatoes, tomato purée, chilli powder, cumin, oregano, salt and pepper and if you're brave, cayenne pepper. Bring to the boil, lower heat, cover the pan and simmer for 45 minutes (or half of Match of the Day!) Stir occasionally.

4. Drain and stir in the kidney beans. Heat for 5 minutes. Serve in big bowls with crusty bread or boiled rice (see page 53).

INGREDIENTS

2 tbls vegetable oil
1 large onion, chopped
2 garlic cloves, chopped
700 g (1½ lbs) lean minced beef
400 g (l lb) tin of tomatoes
2 tbls tomato purée
2 tsps mild chilli powder
1 tsp ground cumin
1 tsp dried oregano
½ tsp salt
Freshly ground black pepper
Pinch of cayenne pepper
(optional – it's HOT, HOT, HOT)
400g (l lb) tin of red kidney beans

ARROZ

GAMES TO PLAY AND EAT

Cooking's no fun.

I prefer playing.

We could make some games to eat.

Dads like to play with their kids but they always need new things to do with them. How about making a great game of draughts. Draw a playing board with 64 squares, 55mm (2¼ inch), on a large sheet of paper and cook the playing pieces. Each time you take an opponent's piece, eat it!

INGREDIENTS

Makes 16
150 g (6 oz) plain chocolate
100 g (4 oz) unsalted butter or margarine, plus 1 tsp
5 eggs
1 tsp vanilla essence
150 g (6 oz) plain flour

¼ tsp salt
100 g (4 oz) cocoa powder
Optional extras: Pecans, walnuts, almonds, hazelnuts, grated orange peel, chocolate chips.

Brownies

To make firm draught pieces, these brownies are baked longer than usual. For gooey ones, cook 5 minutes less.

1. Preheat the oven to 180°C (350°F) or gas mark 4. Grease a 20-22.5 cm (8-9 in) baking tray with the teaspoon of butter.

2. Melt the chocolate and butter together in a heat-proof bowl, either in a microwave set at medium for 2-3 minutes, or by warming the bowl in a half-filled saucepan of simmering water. Wear oven or rubber gloves to protect you from hot steam when you remove the bowl. Leave to cool slightly. If the mixture is too hot the eggs will cook when added.

3. Beat the eggs until frothy and mix in the sugar and vanilla essence. Stir this into the melted chocolate. Slowly add flour, salt and cocoa powder into the mixture.

4. Spread the mixture evenly on to the baking tray and bake for 25-30 minutes.

5. Remove from the oven and allow to cool before cutting out 16 circles (i.e. 12 plus 4 for queening) with a 5 cm (2 in) biscuit cutter.

NOTE Make a wicked ice-cream sundae with the left-over cooked browny. Put some in a tall glass, add ice-cream and top with chocolate sauce.

Whities

These are for the white draught pieces. If cut into squares, this mixture can also be used to make regular Whities.

1. Preheat oven to 180°C (350°F) or gas mark 4. Grease a 20-22.5 cm (8-9 in) baking tray with the teaspoon of butter.

2. Cream together the butter and sugar. Beat into the mixture, the vanilla and almond essence and eggs.

3. Stir in a separate bowl, the flour, ground almonds, baking powder and salt. Then with a wooden spoon, fold (gently mix) it into the egg mixture.

4. Mix in the grated apple.

5. Spread the mixture evenly over the tray and bake for 30 minutes. Remove and allow to cool.

6. When cool, cut into the same size circles as the brownies.

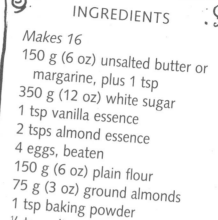

INGREDIENTS

Makes 16
150 g (6 oz) unsalted butter or
    margarine, plus 1 tsp
350 g (12 oz) white sugar
1 tsp vanilla essence
2 tsps almond essence
4 eggs, beaten
150 g (6 oz) plain flour
75 g (3 oz) ground almonds
1 tsp baking powder
¼ tsp salt
1 apple, peeled and grated

Jigsaw Puzzle Cake

This is a simple thin sponge cake iced with a picture then cut into odd shapes to make a jigsaw puzzle.

INGREDIENTS

4 eggs (size 3)
The same weight of:
   Butter or margarine
   Sugar, and
   Self-raising flour
1 tsp vanilla essence

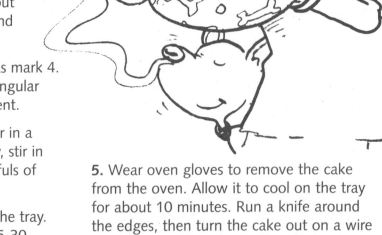

1. Weigh the eggs, then measure out the same weight of butter, sugar and self-raising flour.

2. Set oven at 180°C (350°F) or gas mark 4. Line a 20 x 35 cm (8 x 14 in) rectangular Swiss roll tray with baking parchment.

3. Cream butter and sugar together in a mixing bowl. When light and fluffy, stir in the eggs one at a time with spoonfuls of flour. Add the vanilla essence.

4. Spoon the mixture evenly over the tray. Bake it in the centre of the oven 25-30 minutes until golden brown. Push a thin knife or skewer into the centre of the cake; if it comes out without any goo, it's done.

5. Wear oven gloves to remove the cake from the oven. Allow it to cool on the tray for about 10 minutes. Run a knife around the edges, then turn the cake out on a wire rack, or worktop.

6. Leave the cake to cool completely. If you ice it while it's still warm, the icing will melt.

Easy Icing

Glacé icing is the easiest kind to make.

1. Sift the icing sugar into a bowl.

2. Gradually add the water, stirring briskly with a wooden spoon. Keep stirring until it is smooth and thick enough to coat the back of the spoon without running off. If yours seems too thick, add only the tiniest amount more water (½ teaspoon). This is where most people make the mistake of adding too much water and making the icing too runny.

3. If you want the background of your picture to be coloured, add a few drops of food colouring now and mix in.

4. Use immediately to spread over the cake. Leave to set.

5. When set, use writing icing to draw a picture with lots of things in it.

6. Put the cake in the fridge for an hour to let the icing harden. Then cut the cake into jigsaw shapes and spread them about on a tray. See who can remake the picture fastest.

INGREDIENTS

225 g (8 oz) icing sugar
2 tbls warm water
Food colouring
Writing icing

panic Box

If your icing is too runny, stir in more sifted icing sugar.

A Sandwich Skyscraper

Use a whole loaf of sliced bread to build a giant skyscraper. Make sandwiches with your favourite fillings. Vary the colours to make the different storeys of the building look interesting. Stack them, using cocktail sticks to join them together.

Make a vegetable aeroplane

Popcorn Jewellery

INGREDIENTS

2 tbls oil
100 g (4 oz) popcorn kernels
Thin elastic thread and needle

1. Pour the oil into a large saucepan that has a tight-fitting lid. Put over high heat. When hot, add the corn and cover with lid.

2. Gently shake the pan to coat the corn kernels with oil. As the corn begins to pop, keep shaking the pan to prevent burning.

3. Popcorn is ready when the popping stops. Turn out into a large bowl.

4. When cool, thread corn on to thin elastic thread using a large-eyed needle. Make earrings, bracelets or necklaces.

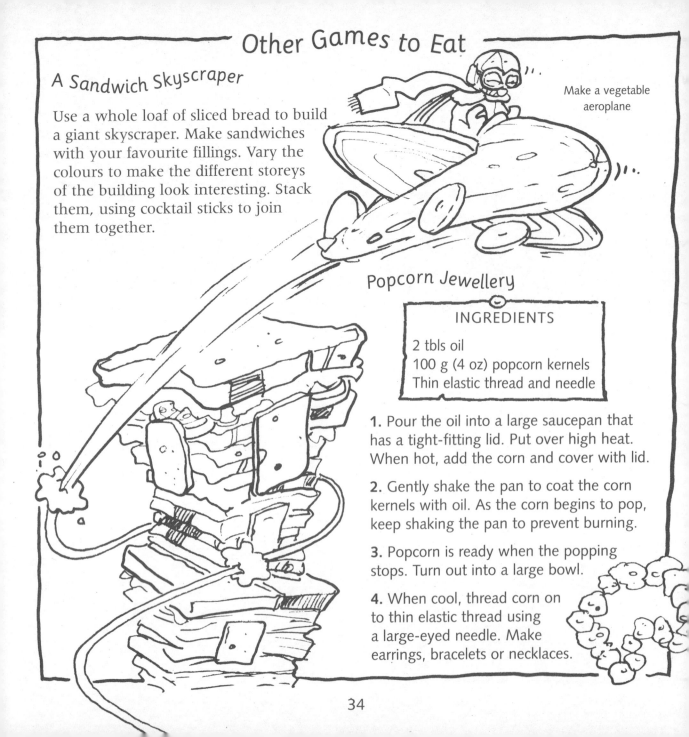

MY DAD'S A CARNIVORE!

Don't you feel guilty eating animals, Dad? According to Animal Aid, in an average life-time a British meat-eater eats 36 pigs, 36 sheep, 8 cows, and 550 birds.*

I don't feel as if I've had a proper meal unless I've had some meat.

Many dads worry that if their children become vegetarians, they won't have a healty diet without meat. But being vegetarian can be very healthy, as long as you eat a balanced and varied diet. Pizza is a favourite meal for both carnivores (meat eaters) and vegetarians. Making your own means you can choose what to put on them. Make double the amount of dough if you want enough pizzas to freeze some for emergency cravings.

Last Green Book on Earth by Judy Allen and Martin Brown, 1994, Red Fox, Random House Children's Books.

Flying Pizzas for Four

INGREDIENTS

For the pizza base
500 g (1 lb) strong
   white flour
1 tsp salt
4 tsps easy blend yeast
2 eggs
2 tbls olive oil
240 ml (8 fl oz) hot
   water
Flour and corn meal

Vegetarian Toppings

Any of these:
Basic tomato sauce (see page 16)
Mozzarella cheese
Vegetarian Cheddar cheese
Olives
Pineapple
Fresh tomato slices
Onion and garlic slices
Red and green peppers
Mushrooms
Sweetcorn
Aubergine (thin slices)
Spinach (cooked and drained)
Egg
Pine nuts
Herbs: oregano, basil, thyme
Pesto sauce
Tomato ketchup

1. Sift the flour, salt and yeast into a large warmed bowl.

2. Mix in the egg, olive oil and hot water to make a dough.

3. Turn out on to a lightly floured surface and knead for 10 minutes. You knead dough by pressing the dough down and forward with your knuckles. Stretch the front of the dough slightly and fold it back towards you.

4. Repeat pressing it down and forward. Turn the dough around from time to time, so that it is worked evenly and will form into a smooth ball. Test the dough by pressing a finger into the middle. If it bounces back leaving hardly any impression, it's ready.

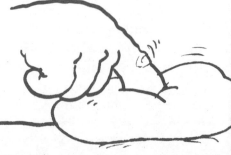

Delicious Combinations

Pineapple and cheese
Mushrooms and garlic
Tomatoes and olives
Tomatoes, cheese, eggs, spinach and peppers
Aubergine, cheese, tomato, more cheese

Panic Box

- If your pizza dough is left too long and goes stringy, make a pizza monster.
- If you overcook your pizza, use it as a dog frisbee. Your dog will probably eat it, then bring it up – the original pavement pizza!

5. Put the dough ball into a lightly-oiled bowl. Cover and leave in a warm place to rise for about 1 hour.

6. Set the oven to 220°C (425°F) or gas mark 7.

7. Knead the dough again until it is smooth and divide it into four. Use a floured rolling pin to roll each piece into a 23 cm (9 inch) disc and place it on a greased baking tray.

8. Brush the top of the dough with oil, then spread over it generous amounts of your chosen toppings. Bake in the oven for 15-20 minutes.

COOKING TIPS
- Bake pizzas two at a time. Assemble two more while the first ones are cooking.
- Oven must be hot before pizza goes in.
- For a crispy base, sprinkle the baking sheet with cornmeal instead of greasing it.

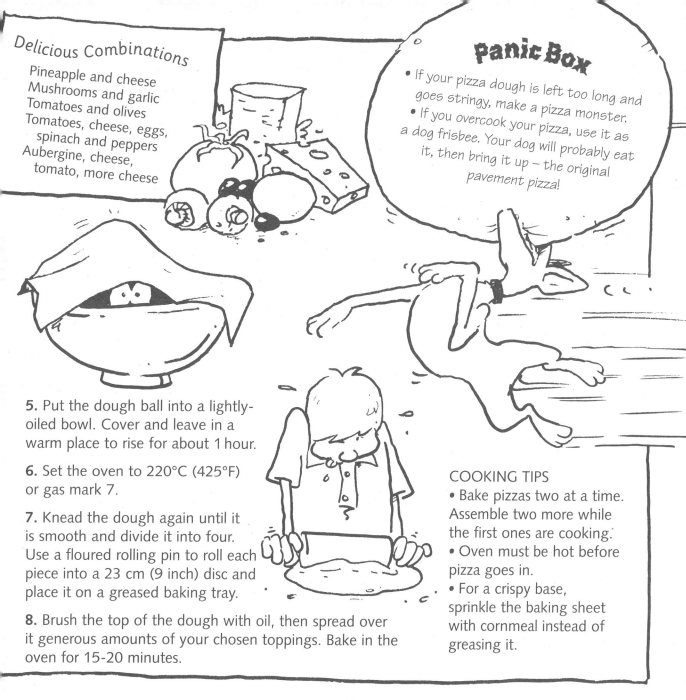

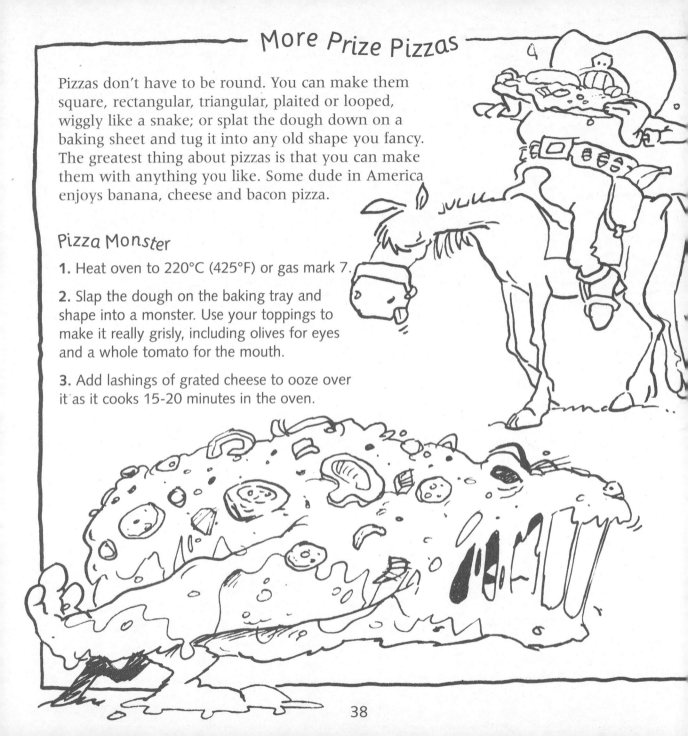

Pizzas don't have to be round. You can make them square, rectangular, triangular, plaited or looped, wiggly like a snake; or splat the dough down on a baking sheet and tug it into any old shape you fancy. The greatest thing about pizzas is that you can make them with anything you like. Some dude in America enjoys banana, cheese and bacon pizza.

Pizza Monster

1. Heat oven to 220°C (425°F) or gas mark 7.

2. Slap the dough on the baking tray and shape into a monster. Use your toppings to make it really grisly, including olives for eyes and a whole tomato for the mouth.

3. Add lashings of grated cheese to ooze over it as it cooks 15-20 minutes in the oven.

Cheat's Pizzas

If you don't want to make pizza dough, buy a bread mix or even a frozen pizza crust. For super-quick pizzas, use crumpets, muffins, pitta bread, bagels, naan, chapati or other Asian breads for the base.

The Double Whammy

Make two pizzas the same size with a different mixture of toppings on each. When they are cooked flip one over the other to make a pizza sandwich!

Pizza Balls

1. Set oven to 220°C (425°F) or gas mark 7.

2. Roll small pieces of dough around cubes of mozzarella cheese. Brush with olive oil and bake for 10 minutes. Or you could make these morish morsels by wrapping up mushrooms or cherry tomatoes and sprinkling them with cheese before cooking.

THE GREAT OUTDOORS

Dad, how did people cook before they had kitchens?

They cooked over open fires. In the wild west, cowboys couldn't just turn on an oven; they had to gather wood and build a fire.

Is that why you like barbecuing? Do you feel like a cowboy

Most dads enjoy cooking on a barbecue. Why not have a real outdoors adventure and make a hungi? That's an underground oven in which you cook a whole meal. In New Zealand, some Maori people still cook hungis for big parties. You will need a whole day to have a hungi – and Dad's help!

NOTE Don't build your hungi in the middle of the lawn. Or you may be hungi, drawn and quartered!

spa

tin foil

3–4 sacks or old towels

wire basket or metal oven rack

newspapers

wood and sticks

24 bri

SAFETY FIRST!
• Don't build your fire under a tree.
• Dad should watch the fire while you prepare the food!

These instructions for building a hungi are adapted from *Two Hundred Years of New Zealand Food and Cooking* by David Bruton, published by Reed in 1982.

How to build a Hungi

1. Wear wellies. Dig a pit in the ground about 40 x 60 cm and 50 cm deep. Pile the earth to one side. Stamp down the soil at the bottom of the pit.

2. Build a bonfire in the pit, starting with crumpled newspaper and kindling (small dry twigs). Pile on wood and any other burnable garden refuse. Don't use any treated wood, it will spoil the taste of the food.

3. Before lighting the fire, flatten the top and pile on the bricks.

4. Dad should light the fire on all four sides so it burns evenly. By the time all the wood has burnt away the bricks will be hot and will have dropped into the base of the pit.

A Hungi for the Hungry

1. Preheat the oven to 190°C (375°F) or gas mark 5.

2. Rub half the garlic into the lamb and season with rosemary, salt and pepper. Rub remaining garlic into the chicken pieces and season with tarragon, salt and pepper. Put all the meat into the oven and cook for 30 minutes to destroy harmful bacteria on the surface.

3. Season vegetables, then wrap them and meat from the oven in individual foil parcels.

4. Put the wrapped lamb and chicken in the wire basket and pile the vegetables on top.

INGREDIENTS

For 12-15 people
1 shoulder of lamb
5 cloves of garlic, peeled and sliced
2 sprigs fresh rosemary or 1 tbl dried rosemary
1 chicken, cut into 8 pieces
2 sprigs fresh tarragon or 1 tsp dried tarragon
12 potatoes, halved
3 sweet potatoes, quartered
12 slices of pumpkin
12 corn on the cob
Salt and pepper

Meanwhile out in the Garden

5. The fire should have burnt down to a few embers with a pile of hot bricks in the middle. Use the spade to spread the bricks out evenly in the pit. Dad could keep a few aside to put on top of the food but be careful, they will be REALLY HOT.

6. Soak sacks in water, wring out, and lay one on top of the bricks in the pit. Lower in the basket.

7. Cover it with a sack and tuck it down the sides. Wrap last sack over it and round the ends. On top, put the hot bricks Dad set aside.

8. Shovel all the earth back into the pit. Trample down well. The hungi will now cook away quietly under-ground and you can do what you like for 3½ hours! Then dig up your grub, unwrap it and tuck in.

Panic Box

• In the unlikely event that it hasn't worked, put the meat back in the oven for up to 1 hour.

• If nosy neighbours complain about the smoke invite them round to sample the delicious food.

Finger-lickin' Barbecued Chicken

Sweet, spicy and sticky barbecued chicken can be eaten hot, then cold the next day. The barbecue sauce keeps for quite a few weeks in the fridge. It's great with meat and vegetables and can be used as a dip as well as a marinade (sauce in which food is soaked to give it a spicy flavour).

SAFETY TIPS
- Always let Dad light the barbecue.
- Never use lighter fluid or any liquid fuel to light a barbecue.
- Never try to pick up hot coals or food with your fingers.

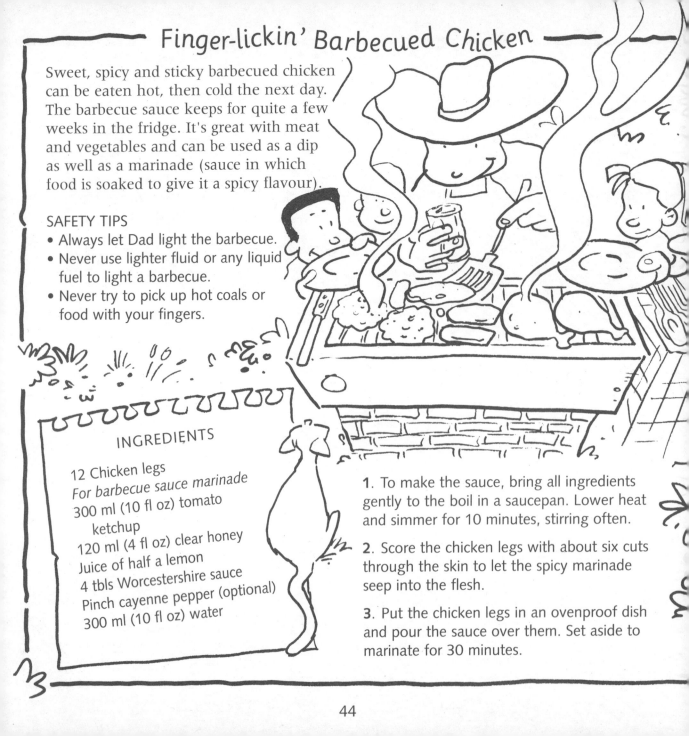

INGREDIENTS

12 Chicken legs
For barbecue sauce marinade
300 ml (10 fl oz) tomato
  ketchup
120 ml (4 fl oz) clear honey
Juice of half a lemon
4 tbls Worcestershire sauce
Pinch cayenne pepper (optional)
300 ml (10 fl oz) water

1. To make the sauce, bring all ingredients gently to the boil in a saucepan. Lower heat and simmer for 10 minutes, stirring often.

2. Score the chicken legs with about six cuts through the skin to let the spicy marinade seep into the flesh.

3. Put the chicken legs in an ovenproof dish and pour the sauce over them. Set aside to marinate for 30 minutes.

More ideas for things to barbecue

Vegetable kebabs. Skewer together and lightly brush with olive oil, any combination of chunks of red, green or yellow peppers, courgettes, aubergines and onions. Cook 5-7 minutes.

New potatoes. Steam or boil, then toss on to the barbecue for 5 minutes to give them a charcoaled flavour.

Corn on the cob. Steam or boil, then brush with oil or some of the barbecue sauce. Cook for 5 minutes, turning occasionally.

Large field mushrooms. Wash, marinate in olive oil, garlic and chopped parsley, then barbecue for 5 minutes.

Haloumi cheese (It's Greek). Cut into 1.5 cm (½ inch) slices and grill on the barbecue for about 3 minutes each side.

Fruit. Try bananas in their skins, halved peaches, slices of pineapple. Heat through.

The guinea pig! Just joking. But did you know that in South America they really do eat them?

4. Preheat the oven to 190°C (375°F) or gas mark 5.

5. Put the chicken legs in the oven and par-cook for 20 minutes while you and Dad prepare and light the barbecue. Alternatively, cover dish with cling film and microwave on high for 10 minutes.

6. Use tongs or a long fork to transfer the chicken legs to the barbecue. Grill them over the hot coals for about 15 minutes. Turn them constantly and baste with the sauce.

COOKING FOR MUM

Cooking for someone is a way of showing you care about them. Mums cook food for the people they love all the time. As well as cooking their favourite food, it's important to present it attractively on the plate and set the table or tray nicely.

> Let's do all the cooking for a day to make mum feel really special.

> She could have breakfast in the bath. Dad will you make a big tray to fit across the bath?

> Good idea!

Mango Hedgehogs

1. Place a ripe (just soft) mango on the worktop and hold it steady. Slice along one side of the stone. Turn the mango over and slice along the other side of the stone. Remove the middle section containing the stone.

2. Cut criss-cross lines, making diamond shapes, into the flesh where the pip was but without cutting through the skin.

3. Push the middle of the skin inside-out on each side of the mango. As you do so, the flesh will make hedgehog prickles.

Mangoes in the Bath

Mangoes are best eaten in the bath where you can let all the juices run down and not worry about the mess.

46

Apple and Cinnamon Bran Muffins

Muffins can be eaten at any time of the day. They are a very popular snack in America. They can be sweet or savoury.

1. Preheat oven to 190°C (375°F) or gas mark 5. Lightly oil 2 x 12-muffin tins, or put paper liners in the muffin cups.

2. Whisk the butter and sugar together in a large bowl until fluffy. Beat in the honey. Beat in the eggs one at a time to make a smooth batter.

3. Sift the flour, baking powder, cinnamon and salt into another bowl and stir in the bran.

4. Gently beat into the batter 2 tablespoons at a time of the flour mixture and the buttermilk. Keep beating them in alternately until used up.

5. Stir in the chopped apple. Fill each muffin cup almost to the top with the mixture.

6. Bake for about 40 minutes, or until puffed up and lightly crusted. Wear oven gloves to take them out of the oven. Cool in the tin for 10 minutes. Serve warm with butter.

INGREDIENTS

Makes 12
2 tsps vegetable oil
225 g (8 oz) unsalted butter
225 g (8 oz) soft brown sugar
120 ml (4 fl oz) runny honey
3 eggs
300 g (10 oz) flour
1 tbls baking powder
2 tsp ground cinnamon
1 tsp salt
300 g (10 oz) unsweetened bran (or Allbran)
300 ml (10 fl oz) buttermilk
3 apples, peeled, cored and chopped

Mother's Day Dilemma

How can Mum spoil her mother if we want to spoil her?

Mum can take her mum out for lunch while we cook the dinner.

What about dad's mum?

MARCH

Invite her for lunch.

Mum

Mum

Morning Dazzler

A real treat to start the day is freshly squeezed orange juice. If you don't have an orange squeezer just cut the oranges in half and use a fork to squidge the juice out.
Or, you can make Mum a Tropical Fizz by mixing some tropical fruit drink with fizzy water.

A Poem for Mum

You could make a card for Mum and write your own special poem in it. Here's one my children wrote for me.

Today we want to cook for you
To show you how we feel.
Just relax, there's nothing to do except enjoy the meal.
Don't worry there's no washing-up to do.
And we hope you don't get ill!

A Giant Biscuit for Mum

Instead of baking Mum a cake, make a giant biscuit that's even bigger than a cake but crispy. You can decorate the top just like a cake, using writing icing and lots of sweeties.

INGREDIENTS

100 g (4 oz) margarine or butter, plus 1 tsp
100 g (4 oz) caster sugar
1 tsp vanilla essence
2 tsps cocoa powder
150 ml (5 fl oz) milk
150 g (6 oz) self-raising flour

100 g (4 oz) chocolate chips
For the decoration
Ready-made or glacé icing (see page 33)
Lots of sweets: Smarties, jelly tots, etc.

1. Preheat the oven to 180°C (350°F), gas mark 4. Grease a loose-bottomed flan or tart dish, with the teaspoon of margarine. You can use a baking tray without a mould but it wouldn't be as round.

2. Cream the margarine and sugar together in a bowl until light and fluffy. Add the vanilla essence, cocoa powder and milk. Mix well.

3. Gradually beat in the flour, then fold in the chocolate chips with a spoon.

4. Spoon the mixture into the flan dish and smooth it to the edges with a spatula. If using a baking tray, spread the mixture on the tray in a circle shape.

5. Bake for 25 minutes. Wear oven gloves to remove it from the oven. Allow to cool 10 minutes before carefully turning it out on to a wire rack.

6. Allow to cool completely (or the icing will melt). Ice the biscuit and decorate it with sweets.

Flower and Nut Salad for Four

Instead of giving mum flowers to put in a vase, you could make her flowers to eat! This dish is perfect for Mum when she's been out to lunch and only wants a little something to nibble on in the evening.

1. Separate the lettuce leaves, wash and dry well and line a large shallow bowl with them. Cut the fruit into segments and arrange over the leaves.

2. Peel and stone the avocado and cut into 8 pieces. Trickle with lemon juice to stop it going brown, then add it to the salad bowl. Sprinkle with rose petals (you can eat them).

3. Beat together with a fork, all the dressing ingredients, then pour it over the salad. Sprinkle with walnuts and serve.

NOTE If you don't have a salad spinner (a contraption that whizzes lettuce round very fast to dry), wrap the leaves in a teatowel and whiz it around your head like a slingshot.

TASTE BUDDIES OF THE ORIENT

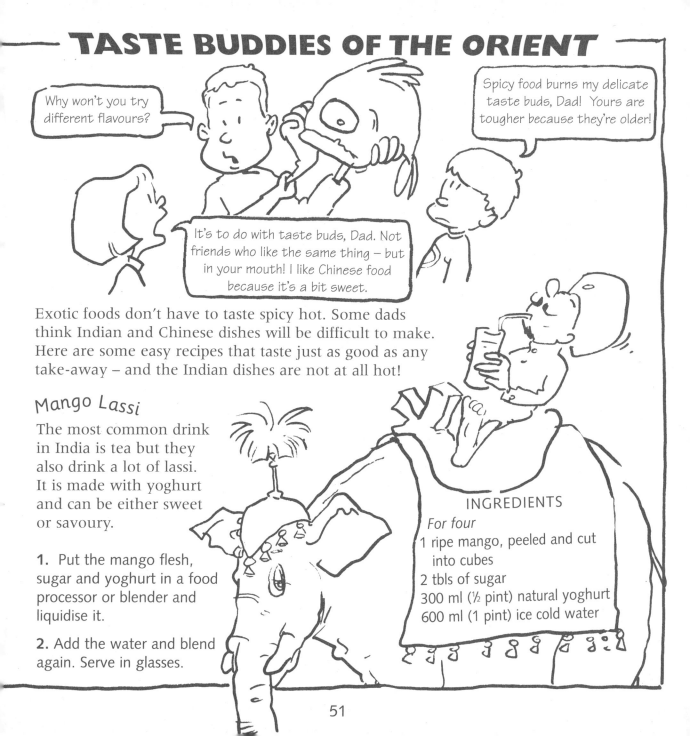

Why won't you try different flavours?

Spicy food burns my delicate taste buds, Dad! Yours are tougher because they're older!

It's to do with taste buds, Dad. Not friends who like the same thing – but in your mouth! I like Chinese food because it's a bit sweet.

Exotic foods don't have to taste spicy hot. Some dads think Indian and Chinese dishes will be difficult to make. Here are some easy recipes that taste just as good as any take-away – and the Indian dishes are not at all hot!

Mango Lassi

The most common drink in India is tea but they also drink a lot of lassi. It is made with yoghurt and can be either sweet or savoury.

1. Put the mango flesh, sugar and yoghurt in a food processor or blender and liquidise it.

2. Add the water and blend again. Serve in glasses.

INGREDIENTS
For four
1 ripe mango, peeled and cut into cubes
2 tbls of sugar
300 ml (½ pint) natural yoghurt
600 ml (1 pint) ice cold water

Chicken Tikka

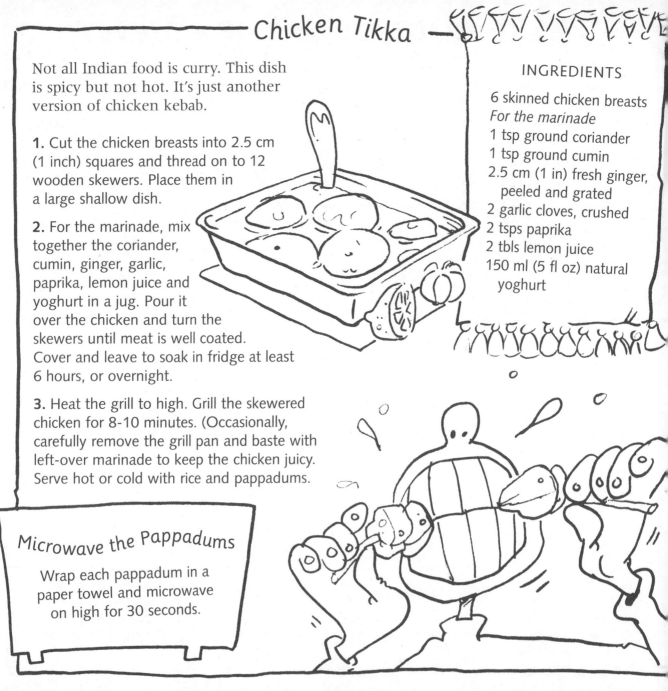

Not all Indian food is curry. This dish is spicy but not hot. It's just another version of chicken kebab.

1. Cut the chicken breasts into 2.5 cm (1 inch) squares and thread on to 12 wooden skewers. Place them in a large shallow dish.

2. For the marinade, mix together the coriander, cumin, ginger, garlic, paprika, lemon juice and yoghurt in a jug. Pour it over the chicken and turn the skewers until meat is well coated. Cover and leave to soak in fridge at least 6 hours, or overnight.

3. Heat the grill to high. Grill the skewered chicken for 8-10 minutes. (Occasionally, carefully remove the grill pan and baste with left-over marinade to keep the chicken juicy. Serve hot or cold with rice and pappadums.

INGREDIENTS

6 skinned chicken breasts
For the marinade
1 tsp ground coriander
1 tsp ground cumin
2.5 cm (1 in) fresh ginger, peeled and grated
2 garlic cloves, crushed
2 tsps paprika
2 tbls lemon juice
150 ml (5 fl oz) natural yoghurt

Microwave the Pappadums

Wrap each pappadum in a paper towel and microwave on high for 30 seconds.

Make Perfect Rice

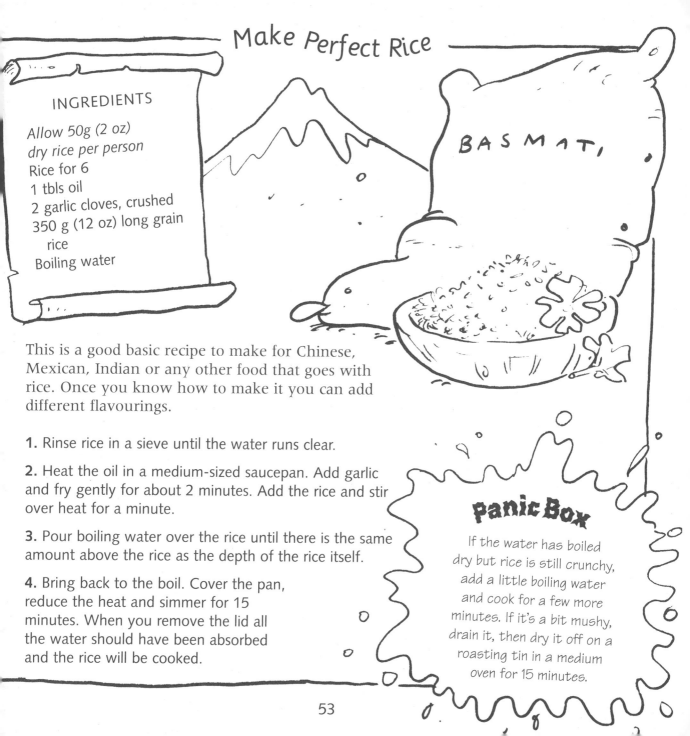

INGREDIENTS

Allow 50g (2 oz)
dry rice per person
Rice for 6
1 tbls oil
2 garlic cloves, crushed
350 g (12 oz) long grain
  rice
Boiling water

This is a good basic recipe to make for Chinese, Mexican, Indian or any other food that goes with rice. Once you know how to make it you can add different flavourings.

1. Rinse rice in a sieve until the water runs clear.

2. Heat the oil in a medium-sized saucepan. Add garlic and fry gently for about 2 minutes. Add the rice and stir over heat for a minute.

3. Pour boiling water over the rice until there is the same amount above the rice as the depth of the rice itself.

4. Bring back to the boil. Cover the pan, reduce the heat and simmer for 15 minutes. When you remove the lid all the water should have been absorbed and the rice will be cooked.

Panic Box

If the water has boiled dry but rice is still crunchy, add a little boiling water and cook for a few more minutes. If it's a bit mushy, drain it, then dry it off on a roasting tin in a medium oven for 15 minutes.

One of the most useful pieces of equipment in any kitchen is a wok. This is a Chinese frying-pan used mainly for stir-frying but you can cook practically anything in it. Stir-frying is great fun. You have to do it *fast* which means the food sometimes spills out all over the place. But it is a quick and healthy way of cooking.

For successful wok cookery

• Season your wok with oil before use – like a cricket bat, though use vegetable oil NOT linseed!

• Heat wok for a few minutes before adding oil for cooking.

• Never immerse your wok in soapy water; just give it a quick scrub then rinse. Dry it immediately and rub a little oil over the inside.

TIPS
• Cut all ingredients the same size.
• Have all your ingredients prepared and in easy reach before you begin. Once you start, you can't stop.
• Start with flavouring ingredients: onions, garlic, ginger etc. Next add those that need the longest cooking, and last, the ingredients that warm through in seconds.

Sweet and Sour Stir-Fry Pork

This is a quick version of Chinese sweet and sour sauce. The pork is not deep-fried and has no red food colouring in it, so it may look different to the one in restaurants but the sauce is really delicious.

1. Mix the cornflour and sherry in a bowl. Add pork. Stir in the pork till well coated. Set aside to marinate for 30 minutes.

2. To make the sauce, mix in a saucepan the cornflour and one tablespoon of soy sauce. Add remaining soy sauce, pineapple chunks and juice, sugar, vinegar and pepper. Bring to the boil. Reduce heat and simmer for 2 minutes, stirring constantly. Remove from heat and set aside.

3. Heat wok over medium heat for about 30 seconds. Add the oil and when it is hot add the pork. Stir-fry the meat for 5-7 minutes, or until it is thoroughly heated through and lightly browned.

4. Add vegetables and stir-fry for 2 minutes.

5. Pour the sauce over it and bring to the boil, stirring all the time. Reduce heat and simmer for 2 minutes. Serve with rice (see page 53).

INGREDIENTS

3 tbls dry sherry
1 tbl cornflour
500 g (1 lb) lean pork, cut into
 1 cm (½ inch) cubes
4 tbls vegetable oil
5 spring onions, chopped,
 cut into 5 cm (2 in) lengths
1 red pepper, de-seeded,
 cut into 5 cm (2 in) strips
For the sauce
1 tbl cornflour
5 tbls soy sauce
3 tbls tinned pineapple chunks
180 ml (6 fl oz) pineapple juice
3 tbls brown sugar
1 tbl white wine vinegar
Freshly ground black pepper

WASHING UP IS A DRAG

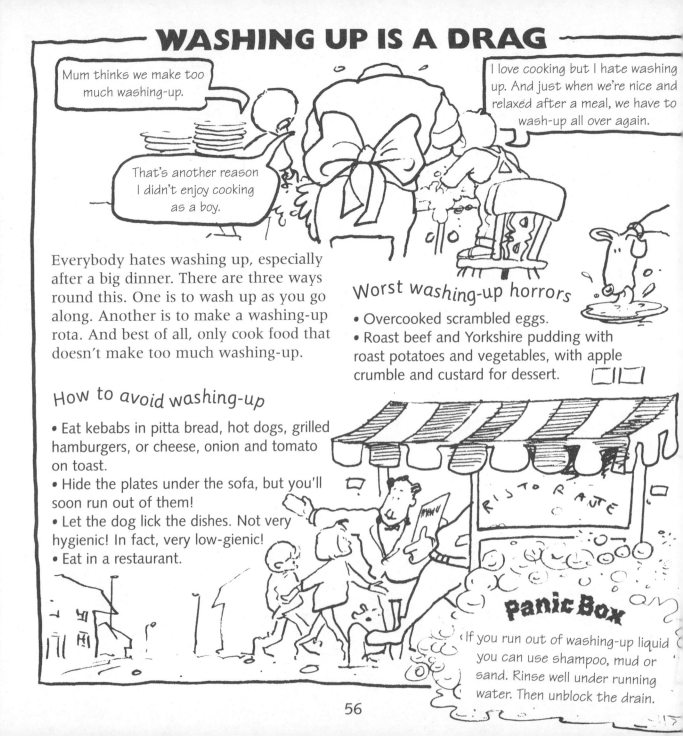

Mum thinks we make too much washing-up.

That's another reason I didn't enjoy cooking as a boy.

I love cooking but I hate washing up. And just when we're nice and relaxed after a meal, we have to wash-up all over again.

Everybody hates washing up, especially after a big dinner. There are three ways round this. One is to wash up as you go along. Another is to make a washing-up rota. And best of all, only cook food that doesn't make too much washing-up.

Worst washing-up horrors

• Overcooked scrambled eggs.
• Roast beef and Yorkshire pudding with roast potatoes and vegetables, with apple crumble and custard for dessert.

How to avoid washing-up

• Eat kebabs in pitta bread, hot dogs, grilled hamburgers, or cheese, onion and tomato on toast.
• Hide the plates under the sofa, but you'll soon run out of them!
• Let the dog lick the dishes. Not very hygienic! In fact, very low-gienic!
• Eat in a restaurant.

Panic Box

If you run out of washing-up liquid you can use shampoo, mud or sand. Rinse well under running water. Then unblock the drain.

Tortilla Rolls for Six

Tortillas are a cross between flat bread and a pancake. They can be folded over, rolled, or used as a sandwich. They are often used in Tex-Mex food, filled with beans, sour cream and guacamole (see page 27).

1. Preheat the oven to 180°C (350°F) or gas mark 4.

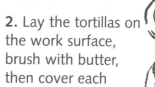

2. Lay the tortillas on the work surface, brush with butter, then cover each one with 2 slices of ham, a good sprinkle of cheese, slices of tomato, a little basil and salt and pepper.

3. Roll up the tortillas, brush with butter, then place join-side-down on a baking sheet. Bake for 15 minutes.

4. Wear oven gloves to transfer tortillas from the oven and on to a plate. Allow to cool slightly. Hold them wrapped in paper napkins to eat.

INGREDIENTS

6 large tortilla flaps
2 tbls melted butter
12 slices honey roast ham
300 g (10 oz) grated
   Cheddar cheese
4 firm tomatoes, sliced
1 tsp dried or fresh basil
Salt and freshly ground
   black pepper

Filo Pastry Pouches

Paper thin squares of filo pastry are really easy to use. You can even use scissors to cut them into shapes. Cover with plastic wrap any pastry you're not working with, as it quickly dries out and becomes unusable.

1. Set oven to 200°C (400°F) or gas mark 6. Lightly oil a baking tray.

2. To make the filling, heat the oil in a large frying pan. Add garlic and onion and cook for 5 minutes. Stir in the spinach and heat.

3. Transfer to a bowl, stir in the ricotta cheese, season with salt and pepper and mix until thoroughly combined. Set aside to cool.

4. Cut the filo pastry into 10 cm (4 in) circles. To assemble the pouches, brush two circles with melted butter, place one on top of the other butter-side up and add a third circle on top. Place a spoonful of the spinach mixture in the centre.

INGREDIENTS

1 pkt frozen filo pastry, thawed
Filling
1 tsp oil
1 garlic clove, crushed
1 onion, finely chopped
150 g (6 oz) frozen spinach, thawed and well drained
150 g (6 oz) ricotta cheese
Salt and pepper to taste
4 tbls melted butter

5. Brush the edges of the pastry with water then draw them up and twist to form a pouch. Brush pouch with butter and put it on a baking tray. Repeat until you've used up all the pastry.

6. Bake for 25 minutes, or until brown.

7. Transfer the pouches to a plate and leave to cool for a few minutes before serving. Eat with your fingers and a paper napkin to catch hot dribbles and crumbs.

TAKING DAD SHOPPING

Shopping can be quite difficult if you're not well organised. Here are some hints for a successful trip to the supermarket. Keep a note of how long it takes and try to beat your record each week.

Super-efficient-market shopping

1. Before you go, try to remember the layout of your local supermarket. Make a map showing where all the items are shelved.

2. Write your shopping list in the order you will pass the shelves.

3. Put soft fruit and vegetables in the front section of trolley to avoid bruising. Unload it last so it goes on top as you take trolley out to car.

4. Never shop when you're hungry.

5. Play BLOGGS! (See page 60.)

BLOGGS! Game Rules

Dad reads out the whole shopping list and you all try to memorise what's on it. Then as you all walk round the supermarket together, the first one to spot an item calls out BLOGGS! The child who spots the most items on the list is the winner and can choose a treat of the week.

BLOGGS!

TIPS FOR DAD

• Test the trolley for wonky wheels before you start.

• Make sure it's always *your* baby in the trolley. Mum will not be pleased if you come home with someone else's!

• Don't let the baby swipe things off the shelves.

TIP FOR KIDS
Keep Dad away from the beer and wine section but steer him *towards* the sweetie and crisp section – especially at the end when he's too fed up to notice.

WHY CAN'T WE EAT AFTERS *BEFORE*?

Wouldn't it be wonderful to plan your own courses and eat whatever you want first. Most families reward their children with pudding after they've eaten the rest of the meal. Dads, why don't you break all the rules and have *afters before*? You probably wanted to when you were a child.

> The Chinese eat soup at the end of a meal. Other people eat sorbet between some courses.

> Why can't we have pudding first? I'd rather have my soup last (if I have any room left).

> Well, I'd like to eat ice-cream for my whole meal.

The Sensible File

There is a good reason for eating dessert last. It's because refined sugar provides loads of calories but contains none of the nutrients necessary to build healthy bodies. Concentrated sweets *seem* to satisfy your appetite, so if you eat sweet things at the beginning of a meal you won't feel hungry enough to eat the foods that are important for you to grow and keep healthy.

Strawberry Ice-cream made in the Garden

Did you know that you can make ice-cream without a freezer?

1. Mash the fruit and sugar with a fork until they are soft and mushy. Mix in the lemon juice and cream. Pour mixture into the small container and close the lid.

2. Put a layer of ice cubes in the bottom of the biscuit tin and sprinkle a layer of salt over them. Put the small container in, then fill the gap around it with more ice and salt.

3. Close the biscuit tin and wrap a towel around it. Leave it in a cool place for 30 minutes.

4. Remove the towel and the two lids. The mixture should have started to freeze around the sides of the inner container. Use a wooden spoon to scrape it down and stir it. This keeps it from freezing solid.

5. Put the lids back on. Cover with a towel and leave until frozen.

6. Remove the towel and lids. Stir the mixture again until it is thick and smooth. Spoon it into bowls and eat it up.

INGREDIENTS

225 g (8 oz) ripe strawberries
100 g (4 oz) caster sugar
Bag of dishwasher salt
Squeeze of lemon juice
300 ml (½ pint) double cream
You will also need
Lots of ice cubes
Large biscuit tin
Smaller container with
    tight-fitting lid
A towel

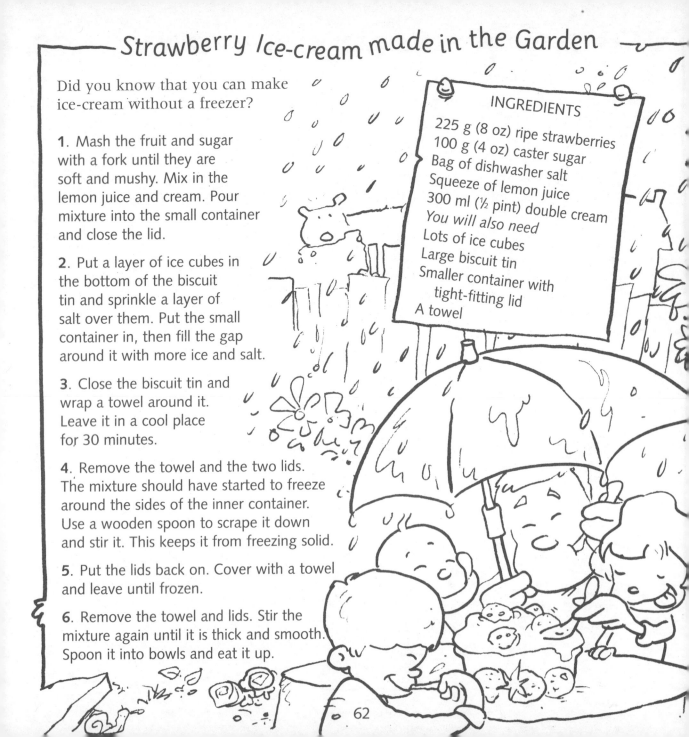

Chocolate Sausage and Mash

You could make a pudding that looks like a savoury course. How about sausage and mash? This is very rich, especially the sausages, so only have one or, at the most, two each! When you cook this dish, make a real sausage and mash for mum. See if you can fool her into thinking you're all eating the same thing.

INGREDIENTS

For the sausages
125 g (6 oz) plain chocolate
100 g (4 oz) unsalted butter
4 tbls double cream
200 g (8oz) icing sugar
2 tbls cocoa powder
For the Gravy
225 g (8 oz) plain chocolate
300 ml (10 fl oz) single cream
For the Mash
Vanilla ice-cream

1. Melt together the chocolate and the butter for the sausages in a small saucepan over low heat, stirring constantly.

2. Remove from heat and stir in the cream until the mixture is smooth. Gradually sift in the icing sugar. Cover and refrigerate for 2 hours.

3. Form into 12 sausage shapes and roll them in cocoa powder. Put them back in the fridge until ready to serve.

4. To make the gravy, melt the chocolate with a few tablespoons of the cream in a double-boiler (see page 5), or in a heatproof bowl set over hot water.

5. When the chocolate has melted, stir in the rest of the cream and keep it warm over the hot water until ready to use.

6. To serve, arrange the sausages and ice-cream mash on a plate and pour the chocolate gravy over them.

Index

Apple and Cinnamon Bran Muffins, 47.

Barbecue: Finger-lickin' Chicken, 44; Ideas for, 45.
Beef, minced: Spaghetti Bolognese, 17; Chilli Con Carne, 29.
Blenders, hand-held, 5, 22.
Bloggs! Game Rules, 60.
Breakfast, 7, 10, 11, 12, 13.
Brownies, 30.
Brunch, 10, 11, 12, 13.

Cakes: Brownies, 30; Whities, 31; Jigsaw Puzzle (sponge) Cake, 32.
Chicken: Finger-lickin' Barbecued, 44; Tikka, 52.
Chilli Con Carne, 29.
Chocolate: Mud Milkshake, 19; Brownies, 30; Giant Biscuit for Mum (chocolate chip cookie), 49; Sausage and Mash, 63.
Cooking can be dangerous, 4.

Desserts: Super-quick Chiffon Pie, 23; Strawberry Ice-cream made in the Garden, 62, Chocolate Sausage and Mash, 63.
Dips: Spinach, 20; White Bean, 21; Guacamole (avocado dip), 27; Mexican Salsa, 28.
Drinks: Morning Dazzler, 48; Mango Lassi, 51, Milkshakes, 19.

Eggs: How to boil, 6; French Toast, 13; Fried, Funny, Daddy's, 7;

Meringues, 8; Separating white from yolk, 8; What to do with six yolks, 9.

Filo Pastry Pouches, 58.
Flower and Nut Salad, 50.

Food Processors, 5, 20.
French Toast, 13.

Guacamole (avocado dip), 27.

Hungi, cooking underground, 40; How to build a Hungi, 41.
Hungi food: lamb, chicken, vegetables, 42-3.

Ice-cream, Strawberry, made in the Garden, 62.
Icing, Easy (glacé), 33.

Jigsaw Puzzle Cake, 32.

Mango: Hedgehogs, 46; Lassi, 51.
Meringues, 8.
Microwave: Cooking Times, 23; Super-quick Chiffon Pie, 23; Pappadums, 52.
Milkshakes: Chocolate Mud, Banana, Other flavours, 19.

Nachos, 26.
Nuts: Flower and Nut Salad, 50.

Outdoor cooking, 40-45, 62.

Pancakes: American, 11; English, 12; Pigs in the Blanket, 13.
Pasta, 14, 15, 16, 17, 18.

Pizza: Flying, 36; Balls, Cheat's, 39; Combinations, 37; Double Whammy, 39; Monster, 38; Vegetarian Toppings, 36.
Popcorn Jewellery, 34.
Pappadums, Microwave the, 52.

Rice, Make Perfect, 53.

Salad, Flower and Nut, 50.
Salsa, Mexican, 28.
Sandwiches: Giant Hero, 25; Skyscraper, 34.
Sausages: Pigs in the Blanket, 13; Chocolate Sausage and Mash, 63.
Shopping, Taking Dad, 59.
Soup, Creamy Leek and Potato, 22.
Spaghetti: Cooking, 15; Tomato Sauce, 16; Bolognese, 17; Coloured Worms with Jam (sweet vermicelli), 18.
Spinach: Filo Pastry Pouches, 58; Dip, 20.
Stir-frying: how to, 54: Sweet and Sour Pork, 55.
Super-quick Chiffon Pie, 23.
Sweet and Sour Stir-fry Pork, 55.

Tools, Terms and Measures, 5.
Tortilla Rolls, 57.

Vegetable Aeroplane, 34.

White Bean Dip, 21.
Whities, 31.
Wokery, Stir-crazy, 54.